PORTRAIT

OF

HEMINGWAY

LILLIAN ROSS

PORTRAIT

OF

HEMINGWAY

THE MODERN LIBRARY

NEW YORK

1999 Modern Library Paperback Edition

Biographical note copyright © 1997 by Random House, Inc.

All rights reserved under International and Pan-American
Copyright Conventions. Published in the United States by
Random House, Inc., New York, and simultaneously in Canada
by Random House of Canada Limited, Toronto.

Modern Library and colophon are registered trademarks
of Random House, Inc.

LIBRARY OF CONGRESS CATALOGING-IN-PUBLICATION DATA
Ross, Lillian, 1927–
Portrait of Hemingway/Lillian Ross
p.   cm.
Previously published: New York: Simon & Schuster, 1961.
ISBN 0-375-75438-5 (acid-free paper)
1. Hemingway, Ernest, 1899–1961.   2. Authors, American—20th
century Biography.   3. Journalists—United States Biography.
I. Title.
PS3515.E37Z77   1999
813'.52—dc21   99-26195
[B]

Modern Library website address: www.modernlibrary.com

Printed in the United States of America

2   4   6   8   9   7   5   3   1

LILLIAN ROSS

Lillian Ross, a writer widely acknowledged as one of today's exemplary literary reporters, was born in Syracuse, New York. Her career in journalism began auspiciously. In 1945 she joined the staff of *The New Yorker*, where she worked with Harold Ross, the magazine's founder and first editor, and over four decades with his successor, the late William Shawn. With Shawn's encouragement, Miss Ross created innovative forms of journalism. One of her earliest pieces, a minute-by-minute account of two days in the life of Ernest Hemingway, presents a unique and vital picture of the novelist. "Portrait of Hemingway," which was originally published as a Profile in *The New Yorker* on May 13, 1950, established her reputation as a journalist who "disappeared" in reports, permitting characters to reveal themselves with their own words and actions.

In the early 1950s Miss Ross went to Hollywood to cover John Huston's filming of *The Red Badge of Courage* for *The New Yorker*. Published in 1952, *Picture* was a breakthrough work, the first piece of factual reporting ever cast in the form of a novel. *Newsweek* called it "the best book on Hollywood ever published." Ernest Hemingway rated *Picture* "much better than most novels," while S. N. Behrman deemed it "the funniest tragedy that I have ever read." And Charlie Chaplin found *Picture* "a brilliant and sagacious bit of reporting rendered in a most disarming style; simple on the surface, yet profound in its choice of incident, which serves to delineate some of the finest bits of characterization written in our time."

But it was William Shawn who so accurately pinpointed Miss Ross's genius as a reporter-writer in *Picture:* "Employing methods of her own invention, Miss Ross demonstrates that although truth is not necessarily stranger than fiction, it can at times arrange itself more artfully. Unimpressed by glamour, undismayed by bar-barism, she looks on impartially and, without passing judgment, coolly sets down what she sees. She possesses a dual gift for invisibility and observation, so that not only does she see, and see profoundly, but people tend to act out their dramas in her presence. Another of her par-ticular gifts is the ability to catch facts on the wing, to describe people in action, to report not on something that happened somewhere before she arrived but on something that was happening while she was there. As if that were not enough, she accomplishes all this with grace, with tact, with humor, even with gaiety, but most important, with understanding."

Over the years, Miss Ross has contributed regularly to *The New Yorker*'s "Talk of the Town" section. Many of these short pieces were later collected in the widely ac-claimed *Talk Stories* (1966) and *Takes* (1983). An early compilation of her work, *Reporting* (1964), has been hailed as a vivid and valuable example of the journalist's art. *Reporting Two* is now in the works. Other books drawn from Miss Ross's articles in *The New Yorker* in-clude *Portrait of Hemingway* (1961), *The Player* (written with her sister, Helen Ross, 1962), *Adlai Stevenson* (1966), and *Moments with Chaplin* (1980). Her satirical short stories about doctors and psychoanalysts were published as the novel *Vertical and Horizontal* (1963). About it, John Updike said: "As a fiction writer Miss Ross begins (with her first novel) as a master."

Following a temporary absence from *The New Yorker*, Miss Ross rejoined the magazine in 1993 to work with editor Tina Brown. Since then she has written a Profile of the actor Tommy Lee Jones and one of actor Robin Williams and his wife, Marsha; "Putting It On," a report on the making of VH1's recent fashion show; and a number of pieces for "The Talk of the Town." "The Shit-Kickers of Madison Avenue," about teenagers on New York's Upper East Side, was published on February 20, 1995, in *The New Yorker*'s seventieth-anniversary issue, and has already become famous.

"Miss Ross's gifts go considerably beyond ordinary journalism," observed Irving Wallace in *The New York Times Book Review*. "She is the mistress of selective listening and viewing, of capturing the one moment that entirely illumines the scene, of fastening on the one quote that Tells All. She is a brilliant interpreter of what she hears and observes. And she is the possessor of a unique writing style—spare, direct, objective, fast—a style that disarms, seemingly only full of wonder, but one that can suddenly, almost sneakily, nail a personality naked to the page. . . . [She is] one of the most creative innocent bystanders of our time."

CONTENTS

PREFACE

I first met Ernest Hemingway on the day before Christmas in 1947, in Ketchum, Idaho. I was on my way back to New York from Mexico, where I had gone to see Sidney Franklin, the American bullfighter from Brooklyn, about whom I was trying to write my first Profile for *The New Yorker*. Hemingway had known Franklin as a bullfighter in Spain in the late twenties and early thirties. I had gone to some *corridas* in Mexico with Franklin, and had been appalled and scared to death when I got my first look at what goes on in a bull ring. Although I appreciated the matador's cape work with the bulls, and the colorful, ceremonial atmosphere, I wasn't fond of bullfighting as such. I guess what interested me was just how Franklin, son of a hard-working policeman in Flatbush, had become a bullfighter. When Franklin told me that Hemingway was the first American who had ever spoken to him intelligently about bullfighting, I telephoned Hemingway in Ketchum. Hemingway liked spending vacations there, skiing and hunting, away from his home in San Francisco de Paula, near Havana, Cuba, and later on he bought a house in Ketchum. When I called, Hemingway was staying in a tourist cabin with his wife, Mary, his sons—John, Patrick, and Gregory—and some fishing friends from Cuba, and he hospitably invited me to drop in and see him on my way back East.

The first time I saw Hemingway was about seven o'clock in the morning, in front of his tourist cabin, shortly after my train got in. He was standing on hard-packed snow, in dry cold of ten degrees below zero, wearing bedroom slippers, no socks, Western trousers with an Indian belt that had a silver buckle, and a light-weight Western-style sports shirt open at the collar and with button-down pockets. He had a graying mustache but had not yet started to wear the patriarchal-looking beard that was eventually to give him an air of saintliness and innocence—an air that somehow or other never seemed to be at odds with his ruggedness. That morning, he looked rugged and burly and eager and friendly and kind. I was wearing a heavy coat, but I was absolutely freezing in the cold. However, Hemingway, when I asked him, said he wasn't a bit cold. He seemed to have tremendous built-in warmth. I spent a wonderful day of talk and Christmas shopping with the Hemingways and their friends. Mary Hemingway, like her husband, was warm and gracious and knowledgeable, as well as capable of brilliantly filling the difficult role of famous writer's wife. She enjoyed the same things he did, and seemed to me to be the perfect partner for him.

Shortly after my Ketchum visit, Hemingway wrote to me from Cuba that he thought I was the person least suited in the world to do an article on bullfighting. Nevertheless, I went ahead, and eventually did finish the Profile of Franklin. After the magazine's editors had accepted it, I sent Hemingway some queries about it, and he replied most helpfully in a letter winding up with the statement that he looked forward with horror to reading it. In the meantime, though, *The New Yorker* published a couple of shorter pieces of mine, and Hemingway and his wife, both regular readers of the magazine (he once wrote me that my mob was his mob, too), seemed to like them. When the Franklin Profile was published, I had a letter from Hemingway, scrawled in pencil, from Villa Aprile, Cortina d'Ampezzo, Italy, in which he said that what he called the Sidney pieces were fine. In his crowded life, he did his best to remember exactly what he had said to you before, and he made a point, generously, of correcting himself when he felt that it was necessary. His compliments were straight and honest, and they were designed to make people feel good. He might call you reliable and compare you to Joe Page and Hugh Casey, and you wouldn't have to be an archivist of baseball to realize you were being praised. The way he wrote in his letters, the way he talked, in itself made me feel good—it was so fresh and wonderful. He was generous in his conversation. He didn't hoard his ideas or his thoughts or his humor of his opinions. He was so inventive that he probably had the feeling there was plenty more where that came from. But whatever his feeling might have been, he would have talked as he did out of sheer generosity. He offered so much in what he said, and always with fun and with sharp understanding and compassion and sensitivity. When he talked, he was free. The sound and the content were marvellously alive.

In the spring of 1950, I wrote a Profile of Hemingway for *The New Yorker*. It was a sympathetic piece, covering two days Hemingway spent in New York, in which I tried to describe as precisely as possible how Hemingway, who had the nerve to be like nobody else on earth, looked and sounded when he was in action, talking, between work periods—to give a picture of the man as he was, in his uniqueness and with his vitality and his enormous spirit of fun intact. Before it was published, I sent a galley proof of it to the Hemingways, and they returned it marked with corrections. In an accompanying letter, Hemingway said that he had found the Profile funny and good, and that he had suggested only one deletion. Then a strange and mysterious thing happened. Nothing like it had ever happened before in my writing experience, or has happened since. To the complete surprise of Hemingway and the editors of *The New Yorker* and myself, it turned out, when the Profile appeared, that what I had written was extremely controversial. Most readers took the piece for just what it was, and I trust that they enjoyed it in an uncomplicated fashion. However, a certain number of readers reacted violently, and in a very complicated fashion. Among these were people who objected strongly to Hemingway's personality, assumed I did the same, and admired the piece for the wrong reasons; that is, they thought that in describing that personality accurately I was ridiculing or attacking it. Other people simply didn't like the way Hemingway talked (they even objected to the playful way he sometimes dropped his articles and spoke a kind of joke Indian language); they didn't like his freedom; they didn't like his not taking himself seriously; they didn't like his wasting his time on going to boxing matches, going to the zoo, talking to friends, going fishing, enjoying people, celebrating his approach to the finish of a book by splurging on caviar and champagne; they didn't like this and they didn't like that. In fact, they didn't like Hemingway to be Hemingway. They wanted him to be somebody else—probably themselves. So they came to the conclusion that either Hemingway had not been portrayed as he was or, if he was that way, I shouldn't have written about him at all. Either they had dreary, small-minded preconceptions about how a great writer should behave and preferred their preconceptions to the facts or they attributed to me their own pious disapproval of Hemingway and then berated me for it. Some of the more devastation-minded among them called the Profile "devastating." When Hemingway heard about all this, he wrote to reassure me. On June 16, 1950, he wrote that I shouldn't worry about the piece and that it was just that people got things all mixed up. A number of times he wrote about the attitude of people he called the devastate people. Some people, he said, couldn't understand his enjoying himself and his not being really spooky; they couldn't understand his being a serious writer without being pompous.

———

Death puts certain things in perspective. No doubt if some of the people who misunderstood the Profile were to read it now, they would see it for what it is. When I wrote the Profile, I attempted to set down only what I had seen and heard, and not to comment on the facts or express any opinions or pass any judgments. However, I believe that today—with the advantage gained by distance—almost any reader would see that although I did not reveal my viewpoint directly, implicit in my choice and arrangement of detail, and in the total atmosphere created, was my feeling of affection and admiration. I liked Hemingway exactly as he was, and I'm content if my Profile caught him exactly as he was during those two days in New York.

While I'm at it, as somebody who has never been concerned with "rating" Hemingway's works but has simply been grateful for whatever joy his writing has offered, I might as well throw in a word about those critics who took an injured, censorious tone when discussing the life that Hemingway led in later years and what they considered a decline in his work. They sometimes sounded as if they thought that Hemingway made a point of letting them, specifically, down, in order to disport himself as a public figure, whereas, as I saw it, he was heroically and uncorruptedly and uncompromisingly occupied day after day with writing as hard as *he could* and as well as *he could* until the day he died. And when he was unable to write or was between books, he still did what *he could*, which was to live life to the full and then, with that limitless generosity of his, make his private experience public, so that everybody else could also have a wonderful time.

Hemingway was generous in so many different ways.

In his letters and in his conversations with friends, Hemingway gave away the very substance out of which another man might have created an entire body of work. The style of Hemingway's letters was a separate style, free and loose and (since he knew that time was short) full of his own shorthand—much freer, as one might expect, than his formal writing. He was a tireless correspondent. I went out to Hollywood for a year and a half after the Profile appeared, to write a series of articles about the making of a movie, and I received scores of letters from Hemingway out there, giving me his views on movies and movie-making and life on the Coast, and also keeping me informed, and entertained, with accounts of his fishing and other adventures in Cuba. When he went to Africa to hunt in 1953, he wrote about the wonders of life there. Africa, he told me, was in many ways the best life of all, and I ought to come there and try it. He usually ended his letters by asking you to write soon. He didn't like to stop writing letters, he once told me, because then he wouldn't receive any, and that would make it lonely. Occasionally, Mary would write a letter, and it would have Hemingway's own kind of enthusiasm and humor. She would write from Kenya that it was the greatest place in the world for waking up in the morning, and that you had to encounter a live, two-ton rhinoceros before dawn, on your way to wash your face, to appreciate what living could be. A lot of other people the Hemingways knew—people who knew them better than I did—probably also got invitations to come there and try it. The Hemingways were always hospitable and friendly. They were always inviting you to visit them in Kenya or in Paris or at their farm in Cuba. I'm sorry that I was never able to do it.

Nobody could fool Hemingway about writing or about writers. He knew both, and he knew them deeply. He knew when a writer was worthless or a fraud, no matter how great the writer's reputation or his sales or his advances from movie companies. About himself he wrote, on August 8, 1950, that all his life he had tried to learn to write better and to know and understand. People, he said, imitated his defects, stole his cadences and rhythms, and called the result the Hemingway school of writing, and nobody wished him well. Then he had an afterthought, and wrote that that was wrong, that a lot of people wished him well but just didn't, he guessed, tell him about it. Writing and literature he took seriously.

And whatever he was asked for he always tried to give. He was quick to respond to younger writers. Once, I asked him to give me a list of reading that he would recommend. He composed the following list:

"Boule de Suif" and "La Maison Tellier"—de Maupassant
"The Red and the Black"—Stendhal
"Les Fleurs du Mal"—Baudelaire
"Madame Bovary"—Flaubert
"Remembrance of Things Past"—Proust
"Buddenbrooks"—Mann
"Taras Bulba"—Gogol
"The Brothers Karamazov"—Dostoevski
"Anna Karenina" and "War and Peace"—Tolstoy
"Huckleberry Finn"—Twain
"Moby Dick"—Melville
"The Scarlet Letter"—Hawthorne
"The Red Badge of Courage"—Crane
"Madame de Mauves"—James

Whatever you brought up with Hemingway, he always tried—or so I found—to give you a response that would be helpful. At one point, after finishing a long piece of work, I told him that I wanted to write shorter and easier pieces from then on. His answer was that I would have to write harder ones and better ones until I died. Only, don't die, he added, explaining that that was the only thing he knew that was really worthless. He was helpful with minor matters, too. When I was in California, trying to learn to ride a horse, Hemingway advised me not to ride any big or fat horses but to get the smallest, smartest, and least mean horse there was. About Hollywood his advice was succinct. He told me not to stay too long.

Hemingway has been called romantic, as distinguished from realistic, about life, especially by some of the heavy thinkers. It always seemed to me that Hemingway was a sound observer and understander of the realities. Once, I passed along some pleasant remarks I had heard about his son John, and Hemingway wrote back that he loved his son very much and then went on to say that in his lifetime he had also loved three continents, several airplanes and ships, the oceans, his sisters, his wives, life and death, morning, noon, evening, and night, honor, bed, boxing, swimming, baseball, shooting, fishing, and reading and writing and all good pictures.

Not long before he died, when he was at the Mayo

Clinic, in Rochester, Minnesota, Hemingway wrote to me that he had his blood-pressure "nonsense" licked again but that he was behind in his work, and that he and Mary were taking off soon for some place where people would leave them alone and "let me write."

—1961

PORTRAIT

OF

HEMINGWAY

ERNEST HEMINGWAY, who may well be the greatest American novelist and short-story writer of our day, rarely comes to New York. For many years, he has spent most of his time on a farm, the Finca Vigia, nine miles outside Havana, with his wife, a domestic staff of nine, fifty-two cats, sixteen dogs, a couple of hundred pigeons, and three cows. When he does come to New York, it is only because he has to pass through it on his way somewhere else. Late in 1949, on his way to Europe, he stopped in New York for a few days. I had written to him asking if I might see him when he came to town, and he had sent me a typewritten letter saying that would be fine and suggesting that I meet his plane at the airport. "I don't want to see anybody I don't like, nor have publicity, nor be tied up all the time," he went on. "Want to go to the Bronx Zoo, Metropolitan Museum, Museum of Modern Art, ditto of Natural History, and see a fight. Want to see the good Breughel at the Met, the one, no two, fine Goyas and Mr. El Greco's Toledo. Don't want to go to Toots Shor's. Am going to try to get into town and out without having to shoot my mouth off. I want to give the joints a miss. Not seeing news people is not a pose. It is only to have time to see your friends." In pencil, he added, "Time is the least thing we have of."

Time did not seem to be pressing Hemingway the day he flew in from Havana. He was to arrive at Idlewild late in the afternoon, and I went out to meet him. His plane had landed by the time I got there, and I found him standing at a gate waiting for his luggage and for his wife, who had gone to attend to it. He had one arm around a scuffed, dilapidated briefcase pasted up with travel stickers. He had the other around a wiry little man whose forehead was covered with enormous beads of perspiration. Hemingway had on a red plaid wool shirt, a figured wool necktie, a tan wool sweater-vest, a brown tweed jacket tight across the back and with sleeves too short for his arms, gray flannel slacks, Argyle socks, and loafers, and he looked bearish, cordial, and constricted. His hair, which was very long in back, was gray, except at the temples, where it was white; his mustache was white, and he had a ragged, half-inch, full white beard. There was a bump about the size of a walnut over his left eye. He had on steel-rimmed spectacles, with a piece of paper under the nosepiece. He was in no hurry to get into Manhattan. He crooked the arm around the brief-case into a tight hug and said that inside was the unfin-ished manuscript of his new book, "Across the River and Into the Trees." He crooked the arm around the wiry lit-tle man into a tight hug and said the man had been his seat companion on the flight. The man's name, as I got it in a mumbled introduction, was Myers, and he was re-turning from a business trip to Cuba. Myers made a slight attempt to dislodge himself from the embrace, but Hemingway held on to him affectionately.

"He read book all way up on plane," Hemingway said. He spoke with a perceptible Midwestern accent, despite the Indian talk. "He liked book, I think," he added, giv-ing Myers a little shake and beaming down at him.

"Whew!" said Myers.

"Book too much for him," Hemingway said. "Book start slow, then increase in pace till it becomes impossible to stand. I bring emotion up to where you can't stand it, then we level off, so we won't have to provide oxygen tents for the readers. Book is like engine. We have to slack off gradually."

"Whew!" said Myers.

Hemingway released him. "Not trying for no-hit game in book," he said. "Going to win maybe twelve to nothing or maybe twelve to eleven."

Myers looked puzzled.

"She's better book than 'Farewell,' " Hemingway said. "I think this is best one, but you are always prejudiced, I guess. Especially if you want to be champion." He shook Myers' hand. "Thanks for reading book," he said.

"Pleasure," Myers said, and walked off unsteadily.

Hemingway watched him go, and then turned to me. "After you finish a book, you know, you're dead," he said moodily. "But no one knows you're dead. All they see is the irresponsibility that comes in after the terrible responsibility of writing." He said he felt tired but was in good shape physically; he had brought his weight down to two hundred and eight, and his blood pressure was down, too. He had considerable rewriting to do on his book, and he was determined to keep at it until he was absolutely satisfied. "They can't yank novelist like they can pitcher," he said. "Novelist has to go the full nine, even if it kills him."

We were joined by Hemingway's wife, Mary, a small, energetic, cheerful woman with close-cropped blond hair, who was wearing a long, belted mink coat. A porter pushing a cart heaped with luggage followed her. "Papa, everything is here," she said to Hemingway. "Now we ought to get going, Papa." He assumed the air of a man who is not going to be rushed. Slowly, he counted the pieces of luggage. There were fourteen, half of them, Mrs. Hemingway told me, extra-large Valpaks designed by her husband and bearing their *hierro,* also designed by him. When Hemingway had finished counting, his wife suggested that he tell the porter where to put the luggage. Hemingway told the porter to stay right there and watch it; then he turned to his wife and said, "Let's not crowd, honey. Order of the day is to have a drink first."

We went into the airport cocktail lounge and stood at the bar. Hemingway put his briefcase down on a chromium stool and pulled the stool close to him. He ordered bourbon and water. Mrs. Hemingway said she would have the same, and I ordered a cup of coffee. Hemingway told the bartender to bring double bourbons. He waited for the drinks with impatience, holding on to the bar with both hands and humming an unrecognizable tune. Mrs. Hemingway said she hoped it wouldn't be dark by the time they got to New York. Hemingway said it wouldn't make any difference to him, because New York was a rough town, a phony town, a town that was the same in the dark as it was in the light, and he was not exactly overjoyed to be going there anyway. What he was looking forward to, he said, was Venice. "Where I like it is out West in Wyoming, Montana, and Idaho, and I like Cuba and Paris and around Venice," he said. "Westport gives me the horrors." Mrs. Hemingway lit a cigarette and handed me the pack. I passed it along to him, but he said he didn't smoke. Smoking ruined his sense of smell, a sense he found completely indispensable for hunting. "Cigarettes smell so awful to you when you have a nose that can truly smell," he said, and laughed, hunching his shoulders and raising the back of his fist to his face, as though he expected somebody to hit him. Then he enumerated elk, deer, possum, and coon as some of the things he could truly smell.

The bartender brought the drinks. Hemingway took several large swallows and said he got along fine with animals, sometimes better than with human beings. In Montana, once, he lived with a bear, and the bear slept with him, got drunk with him, and was a close friend. He asked me whether there were still bears at the Bronx Zoo, and I said I didn't know but I was pretty sure there were bears at the Central Park Zoo. "I always used to go to the Bronx Zoo with Granny Rice," he said. "I love to go to the zoo. But not on Sunday. I don't like to see the people making fun of the animals, when it should be the other way around." Mrs. Hemingway took a small notebook out of her purse and opened it; she told me she had made a list of chores she and her husband had to do before their boat sailed. They included buying a hot-water-bottle cover, an elementary Italian grammar, a short history of Italy, and, for Hemingway, four woollen undershirts, four pairs of cotton underpants, two pairs of woollen underpants, bedroom slippers, a belt, and a coat. "Papa has never had a coat," she said. "We've got to buy

Papa a coat." Hemingway grunted and leaned against the bar. "A nice, rainproof coat," Mrs. Hemingway said. "And he's got to get his glasses fixed. He needs some good, soft padding for the nosepiece. It cuts him up brutally. He's had that same piece of paper under the nosepiece for weeks. When he really wants to get cleaned up, he changes the paper." Hemingway grunted again.

The bartender came up, and Hemingway asked him to bring another round of drinks. Then he said, "First thing we do, Mary, as soon as we hit hotel, is call up the Kraut." "The Kraut," he told me, with that same fist-to-the-face laugh, was his affectionate term for Marlene Dietrich, an old friend, and was part of a large vocabulary of special code terms and speech mannerisms indigenous to the Finca Vigia. "We have a lot of fun talking a sort of joke language," he said.

"First we call Marlene, and then we order caviar and champagne, Papa," Mrs. Hemingway said. "I've been waiting months for that caviar and champagne."

"The Kraut, caviar, and champagne," Hemingway said slowly, as though he were memorizing a difficult set of military orders. He finished his drink and gave the bartender a repeat nod, and then he turned to me. "You want to go with me to buy coat?" he asked.

"Buy coat and get glasses fixed," Mrs. Hemingway said.

I said I would be happy to help him do both, and then I reminded him that he had said he wanted to see a fight. The only fight that week, I had learned from a friend who knows all about fights, was at the St. Nicholas Arena that night. I said that my friend had four tickets and would like to take all of us. Hemingway wanted to know who was fighting. When I told him, he said they were bums. Bums, Mrs. Hemingway repeated, and added that they had better fighters in Cuba. Hemingway gave me a long, reproachful look. "Daughter, you've got to learn that a bad fight is worse than no fight," he said. We would all go to a fight when he got back from Europe, he said, because it was absolutely necessary to go to several good fights a year. "If you quit going for too long a time, then you never go near them," he said. "That would be very dangerous." He was interrupted by a brief fit of coughing. "Finally," he concluded, "you end up in one room and won't move."

After dallying at the bar a while longer, the Hemingways asked me to go with them to their hotel. Hemingway ordered the luggage loaded into a taxi, and the three of us got into another. It was dark now. As we drove along the boulevard, Hemingway watched the road carefully. Mrs. Hemingway told me that he always watched the road, usually from the front seat. It was a habit he had got into during the First World War. I asked them what they planned to do in Europe. They said they were going to stay a week or so in Paris and then drive to Venice.

"I love to go back to Paris," Hemingway said, his eyes still fixed on the road. "Am going in the back door and have no interviews and no publicity and never get a haircut, like in the old days. Want to go to cafés where I know no one but one waiter and his replacement, see all the new pictures and the old ones, go to the bike races and the fights, and see the new riders and fighters. Find good, cheap restaurants where you can keep your own napkin. Walk all over the town and see where we made our mistakes and where we had our few bright ideas. And learn the form and try and pick winners in the blue, smoky afternoons, and then go out the next day to play them at Auteuil and Enghien."

"Papa is a good handicapper," Mrs. Hemingway said.

"When I know the form," he said.

We were crossing the Queensboro Bridge, and we had a clear view of the Manhattan skyline. The lights were on in the tall office buildings. Hemingway did not seem to be impressed. "This ain't my town," he said. "It's a town you come to for a short time. It's murder." Paris was like another home to him, he said. "I am as lonesome and as happy as I can be in that town we lived in and worked and learned and grew up in, and then fought our way back into." Venice was another of his home towns. The last time he and his wife were in Italy, they had lived for four months in Venice and the Cortina Valley, and he had gone hunting, and now he had put the locale and some of the people in the book he was writing. "Italy was so damned wonderful," he said. "It was sort of like having died and gone to Heaven, a place you'd figured never to see."

Mrs. Hemingway said that she had broken her right ankle skiing there but that she planned to go skiing there again. Hemingway had been hospitalized in Padua with an eye infection, which developed into erysipelas, but he wanted to go back to Italy and wanted to see his many good friends there. He was looking forward to seeing the gondoliers on a windy day, the Gritti Palace Hotel, where they stayed during their last visit, and the Locanda Cipriani, which was an old inn on Torcello, an island in the lagoon northeast of Venice where some of the original Venetians lived before they built Venice. Now about seventy people lived on Torcello, and the men were professional duckhunters. While there, Hemingway had gone duckhunting a lot with the gardener of the old inn. "We'd go around through the canals and jumpshoot, and I'd walk the prairies at low tide for snipe," he said. "It was a big fly route for ducks that came all the way down from the Pripet Marshes. I shot good and thus became a respected local character. They have some sort of little bird that comes through, after eating grapes in the north, on his way to eat grapes in the south. The local characters sometimes shot them sitting, and I occasionally shot them flying. Once, I shot two high doubles, rights and lefts, in a row, and the gardener cried with emotion. Coming home, I shot a high duck against the rising moon and dropped him in the canal. That precipitated an emotional crisis I thought I would never get him out of but did, with about a pint of Chianti. We each

took a pint out with us. I drank mine to keep warm com-
ing home. He drank his when overcome by emotion."
We were silent for a while, and then Hemingway said,
"Venice was lovely."

—

The Hemingways were stopping at the Sherry-
Netherland. Hemingway registered and told the room
clerk that he did not want any announcement made of
his arrival and did not want any visitors, or any telephone calls, either, except from Miss Dietrich. Then we
went up to the suite—living room, bedroom, and serving pantry—that had been reserved for them. Hemingway paused at the entrance and scouted the living room.
It was large, decorated in garish colors, and furnished
with imitation-Chippendale furniture and an imitation
fireplace containing imitation coals.

"Joint looks O.K.," he said. "Guess they call this the
Chinese Gothic Room." He moved in and took the
room.

Mrs. Hemingway went over to a bookcase and exam-
ined its contents. "Look, Papa," she said. "They're phony.
They're pasteboard backs, Papa. They're not real books."

Hemingway put his briefcase down on a bright-red

couch and advanced on the bookcase, then slowly, with expression, read the titles aloud—"Elementary Economics," "Government of the United States," "Sweden, the Land and the People," and "Sleep in Peace," by Phyllis Bentley. "I think we are an outfit headed for extinction," he said, starting to take off his necktie.

After getting his necktie off, and then his jacket, Hemingway handed them to his wife, who went into the bedroom, saying she was going to unpack. He unbuttoned his collar and went over to the telephone. "Got to call the Kraut," he said. He telephoned the Plaza and asked for Miss Dietrich. She was out, and he left word for her to come over for supper. Then he called room service and ordered caviar and a couple of bottles of Perrier-Jouët, *brut*.

Hemingway went back to the bookcase and stood there stiffly, as though he could not decide what to do with himself. He looked at the pasteboard backs again and said, "Phony, just like the town." I said that there was a tremendous amount of talk about him these days in literary circles—that the critics seemed to be talking and writing definitively not only about the work he had done but about the work he was going to do. He said that, of all the people he did not wish to see in New York, the people he wished least to see were the critics. "They are like those people who go to ball games and can't tell the players without a score card," he said. "I am not worried about what anybody I do not like might do. What the hell! If they can do you harm, let them do it. It is like being a third baseman and protesting because they hit line drives to you. Line drives are regrettable, but to be expected." The closest competitors of the critics among those he wished least to see, he said, were certain writers who wrote books about the war when they had not seen anything of war at first hand. "They are just like an outfielder who will drop a fly on you when you have pitched to have the batter hit a high fly to that outfielder, or when they're pitching they try to strike everybody out." When he pitched, he said, he never struck anybody out, except under extreme necessity. "I knew I had only so many fast balls in that arm," he said. "Would make them pop to short instead, or fly out, or hit it on the ground, bouncing."

A waiter arrived with the caviar and champagne, and Hemingway told him to open one of the bottles. Mrs. Hemingway came in from the bedroom and said she

18 · *Lillian Ross*

couldn't find his toothbrush. He said that he didn't know where it was but that he could easily buy another. Mrs. Hemingway said all right, and went back into the bedroom. Hemingway poured two glasses of champagne, gave one to me, and picked up the other one and took a sip. The waiter watched him anxiously. Hemingway hunched his shoulders and said something in Spanish to the waiter. They both laughed, and the waiter left. Hemingway took his glass over to the red couch and sat down, and I sat in a chair opposite him.

"I can remember feeling so awful about the first war that I couldn't write about it for ten years," he said, suddenly very angry. "The wound combat makes in you, as a writer, is a very slow-healing one. I wrote three stories about it in the old days—'In Another Country,' 'A Way You'll Never Be,' and 'Now I Lay Me.' " He mentioned a war writer who, he said, was apparently thinking of himself as Tolstoy, but who'd be able to play Tolstoy only on the Bryn Mawr field-hockey team. "He never hears a shot fired in anger, and he sets out to beat who? Tolstoy, an artillery officer who fought at Sevastopol, who knew his stuff, who was a hell of a man anywhere you put him—bed, bar, in an empty room where he had to think. I started out very quiet and I beat Mr. Turgenev. Then I trained hard and I beat Mr. de Maupassant. I've fought two draws with Mr. Stendhal, and I think I had an edge in the last one. But nobody's going to get me in any ring with Mr. Tolstoy unless I'm crazy or I keep getting better."

He had begun his new book as a short story. "Then I couldn't stop it. It went straight on into a novel," he said. "That's the way all my novels got started. When I was twenty-five, I read novels by Somersault Maugham and Stephen St. Vixen Benét." He laughed hoarsely. "They had written novels, and I was ashamed because I had not written any novels. So I wrote 'The Sun' when I was twenty-seven, and I wrote it in six weeks, starting on my birthday, July 21st, in Valencia, and finishing it September 6th, in Paris. But it was really lousy and the rewriting took nearly five months. Maybe that will encourage young writers so they won't have to go get advice from their psychoanalysts. Analyst once wrote me, What did I learn from psychoanalysts? I answered, Very little but hope they had learned as much as they were able to understand from my published works. You never saw a counter-puncher who was punchy. Never lead against a hitter unless you can outhit him. Crowd a boxer, and take everything he has, to get inside. Duck a swing. Block a hook. And counter a jab with everything you own. Papa's delivery of hard-learned facts of life."

Hemingway poured himself another glass of champagne. He liked to write in longhand, he said, but he had recently bought a tape recorder and was trying to get up the courage to use it. "I'd like to learn talk machine," he said. "You just tell talk machine anything you want and get secretary to type it out." He wrote without facility, except for dialogue. "When the people are talking, I can hardly write it fast enough or keep up with it, but with an almost unbearable high manifold pleasure. I put more inches on than she will take, and then fly her as near as I know to how she should be flown, only flying as crazy as really good pilots fly crazy sometimes. Most of the time flying conservatively but with an awfully fast airplane that makes up for the conservatism. That way, you live longer. I mean your writing lives longer. How do you like it now, gentlemen?" The question seemed to have some special significance for him, but he did not bother to explain it.

I wanted to know whether, in his opinion, the new book was different from his others, and he gave me another long, reproachful look. "What do you think?" he said after a moment. "You don't expect me to write 'The Farewell to Arms Boys in Addis Ababa,' do you? Or 'The Farewell to Arms Boys Take a Gunboat'?" The book was about the command level in the Second World War. "I am not interested in the G.I. who wasn't one," he said, suddenly angry again. "Or the injustices done to *me*, with a capital 'M.' I am interested in the goddam sad science of war." The new novel had a good deal of profanity in it. "That's because in war they talk profane, although I always try to talk gently," he said. "I think I've got 'Farewell' beat in this one," he went on. He touched his briefcase. "It hasn't got the youth and the ignorance." Then he asked wearily, "How do you like it now, gentlemen?"

There was a knock at the door, and Hemingway got up quickly and opened it. It was Miss Dietrich. Their reunion was a happy one. Mrs. Hemingway came out of the bedroom and greeted the guest enthusiastically. Miss

Dietrich stood back from Hemingway and looked at him with approval. "Papa, you look wonderful," she said slowly.

"I sure missed you, daughter," said Hemingway. He raised his fist to his face, and his shoulders shook as he laughed silently.

Miss Dietrich was wearing a mink coat. She sighed loudly, took off the coat, and handed it to Mrs. Hemingway. Then she sighed again and sat down in an overstuffed chair. Hemingway poured a glass of champagne, took it to her, and refilled the other glasses.

"The Kraut's the best that ever came into the ring," he said as he handed me my glass. Then he pulled a chair up beside Miss Dietrich's, and they compared notes on friends and on themselves. They talked about theatre and motion-picture people, one of whom, a man, Hemingway referred to as a "sea heel."

Miss Dietrich wanted to know what a sea heel was.

"The sea is bigger than the land," he told her.

Mrs. Hemingway went into the serving pantry and came out in a few minutes with caviar spread on toast.

"Mary, I am telling Papa how I have to behave because I am a grandmother," Miss Dietrich said, taking a piece of toast. "I have to think always of the children. You know, Papa?"

Hemingway gave a sympathetic grunt, and Miss Dietrich took from her purse some snapshots of her grandson and passed them around. He was eighteen months old, she told us. Hemingway said that he looked like a winner, and that he would be proud to own a piece of him if he ever got into the ring.

Miss Dietrich said that her daughter was going to have another child soon. "I'll be a grandmother *again*, Papa," she said.

Hemingway gave her a bleak look. "I'm going to be a grandfather in a few months," he said. "My son Bumby's wife."

Mrs. Hemingway told me that Bumby was the nickname of her husband's eldest son, John, an Army captain stationed in Berlin. His two other sons, she said, were Patrick, known as Mouse, who was a twenty-one-year-old sophomore at Harvard, and was planning to get married in June, and Gregory, known as Gigi, who was eighteen and a freshman at St. John's, at Annapolis. In addition to the present Mrs. Hemingway, Patrick was going to invite to his wedding his and Gigi's mother,

Pauline Pfeiffer, who was Hemingway's second wife. Bumby's mother and Hemingway's first wife was Hadley Richardson, now Mrs. Paul Scott Mowrer, and Hemingway's third wife was Martha Gellhorn.

"Everything you do, you do for the sake of the children," Miss Dietrich said.

"Everything for the children," Hemingway said. He refilled Miss Dietrich's glass.

"Thank you, Papa," she said, and sighed. She lived at the Plaza, she told him, but spent a good deal of her time at the apartment of her daughter, who lived on Third Avenue. "Papa, you should see me when they go out," she said, and took a sip of champagne. "I'm the baby-sitter. As soon as they leave the house, I go around and look in all the corners and straighten the drawers and clean up. I can't stand a house that isn't neat and clean. I go around in all the corners with towels I bring with me from the Plaza, and I clean up the whole house. Then they come home at one or two in the morning, and I take the dirty towels and some of the baby's things that need washing, and, with my bundle over my shoulder, I go out and get a taxi, and the driver, he thinks I am this old washerwoman from Third Avenue, and he takes me in the taxi and talks to me with sympathy, so I am afraid to let him take me to the Plaza. I get out a block away from the Plaza and I walk home with my bundle and I wash the baby's things, and then I go to sleep."

"Daughter, you're hitting them with the bases loaded," Hemingway said earnestly.

There was a ring at the door, and a bellboy brought in a florist's box. Mrs. Hemingway opened it and took out some green orchids, which were from her mother. Mrs. Hemingway put the flowers in a vase and said it was time to order supper.

As we ate, the Hemingways and Miss Dietrich talked about the war. All three had seen it at first hand. Mrs. Hemingway, who, as Mary Welsh, was a *Time* correspondent in London, met Hemingway there during the war, and both saw a good deal of Miss Dietrich there and, later on, in Paris. Miss Dietrich was a U.S.O. entertainer, and performed on almost every front in the European theatre. She grew a little sad as she talked about the war. She had loved entertaining the troops, and the spirit overseas, she said, was the best she had ever found in people anywhere. "Everybody was the way people should be all the time," she continued. "Not mean and afraid but good to each other."

Hemingway raised his glass in a toast to her.

"I've finally figured out why Papa sometimes gets mean now that the war is over," Mrs. Hemingway said. "It's because there is no occasion for him to be valorous in peacetime."

"It was different in the war," Miss Dietrich said. "People were not so selfish and they helped each other."

Hemingway asked her about some recordings she had made, during the war, of popular American songs with lyrics translated into German, and said he'd like to have them. "I'll give you manuscript of new book for recordings if you want to trade even, daughter," he told her.

"Papa, I don't trade with you. I love you," said Miss Dietrich.

"You're the best that ever came into the ring," Hemingway said.

———

Late the next morning, I was awakened by a telephone call from Hemingway, who asked me to come right over to the hotel. He sounded urgent. I had a fast cup of coffee, and when I arrived at the suite, I found the door open and walked in. Hemingway was talking on the telephone. He was wearing an orange plaid bathrobe that looked too small for him, and he had a glass of champagne in one hand. His beard looked more scraggly than it had the day before. "My boy Patrick is coming down from Harvard and I'd like to reserve a room for him," he was saying into the telephone. " 'P,' as in 'Patrick.' " He paused and took a sip of champagne. "Much obliged. He'll be down from Harvard."

Hemingway hung up and, from his bathrobe pocket, took a box of pills. He shook two of them into the palm of his hand and downed them with a mouthful of champagne. He told me that he had been up since six, that his wife was still asleep, and that he had done enough work for that morning and wanted to talk, an activity he found relaxing. He always woke at daybreak, he explained, because his eyelids were especially thin and his eyes especially sensitive to light. "I have seen all the sunrises there have been in my life, and that's half a hundred years," he said. He had done considerable revision that morning on the manuscript. "I wake up in the morning and my mind starts making sentences, and I have to get rid of them fast—talk them or write them down," he said. "How did you like the Kraut?"

"Very much," I said.

"I love the Kraut and I love Ingrid," he said. "If I weren't married to Miss Mary and didn't love Miss Mary, I would try to hook up with either of them. Each one has what the other hasn't. And what each has, I love very much." For a moment, he looked bewildered, and then he said quickly, "Would never marry an actress, on account they have their careers and they work bad hours."

I asked him whether he still wanted to buy a coat, and he said sure but he didn't want to be rushed or crowded and it was cold outside. On a serving table near the couch were two champagne coolers, each containing ice and a bottle. He carried his glass over there and held up one of the bottles and squinted at it. It was empty. He put it back in the cooler, head down. Then he opened the other bottle, and as he poured some champagne into his glass, he sang, " 'So feed me am-mu-nition, keep me in the Third Division, your dog-face soldier boy's O.K.' " Breaking off, he said, "Song of the Third Infantry Division. I like this song when I need music inside myself to go on. I love all music, even opera. But I have no talent for it and cannot sing. I have a perfect goddam ear for music, but I can't play any instrument by ear—not even the piano. My mother used to make me play the cello. She took me out of school one year to learn the cello, when I wanted to be out in the fresh air playing football. She wanted to have chamber music in the house."

His briefcase was lying open on a chair near the desk, and the manuscript pages were protruding from it; someone seemed to have stuffed them into the briefcase without much care. Hemingway told me that he had been cutting the manuscript. "The test of a book is how much good stuff you can throw away," he said. "When I'm writing it, I'm just as proud as a goddam lion. I use the oldest words in the English language. People think I'm an ignorant bastard who doesn't know the ten-dollar words. I know the ten-dollar words. There are older and better words which if you arrange them in the proper combination you make it stick. Remember, anybody who pulls his erudition or education on you hasn't any. Also, daughter, remember that I never carried Teddy bears to bed with me since I was four. Now, with seventy-eight-year-old grandmothers taking advantage of loopholes in the G.I. Bill of Rights whereby a gold-star mother can receive her son's education, I thought of establishing a scholarship and sending myself to Harvard, because my Aunt Arabelle has always felt very bad that I am the only Hemingway boy that never went to college. But I have been so busy I have not got around to it. I only went to high school and a couple of military cram courses, and never took French. I began to learn to read French by reading the A.P. story in the French paper after reading the American A.P. story, and finally learned to read it by reading accounts of things I had seen—*les événements sportifs*—and from that and *les crimes* it was only a jump to Dr. de Maupassant, who wrote about things I had seen or could understand. Dumas, Daudet, Stendhal, who when I read him I knew that was the way I wanted to be able to write. Mr. Flaubert, who always threw them perfectly straight, hard, high, and inside. Then Mr. Baudelaire, that I learned my knuckle ball from, and Mr. Rimbaud, who never threw a fast ball in his life. Mr. Gide and Mr. Valéry I couldn't learn from. I think Mr. Valéry was too smart for me. Like Jack Britton and Benny Leonard."

Jack Britton, he continued, was a fighter he admired

very much. "Jack Britton kept on his toes and moved around and never let them hit him solid," he said. "I like to keep on my toes and never let them hit me solid. Never lead against a hitter unless you can outhit him. Crowd a boxer," he said, assuming a boxing stance and holding his right hand, which was grasping the champagne glass, close to his chest. With his left hand, he punched at the air, saying, "Remember. Duck a swing. Block a hook. And counter a jab with everything you own." He straightened up and looked thoughtfully at his glass. Then he said, "One time, I asked Jack, speaking of a fight with Benny Leonard, 'How did you handle Benny so easy, Jack?' 'Ernie,' he said, 'Benny is an awfully smart boxer. All the time he's boxing, he's thinking. All the time he was thinking, I was hitting him.' " Hemingway gave a hoarse laugh, as though he had heard the story for the first time. "Jack moved very geometrically pure, never one hundredth of an inch too much. No one ever got a solid shot at him. Wasn't anybody he couldn't hit any time he wanted to." He laughed again. " 'All the time he was thinking, I was hitting him.' " The anecdote, he told me, had been in the original version of his short story "Fifty Grand," but Scott Fitzgerald had persuaded him to take it out. "Scott thought everybody knew about it, when only Jack Britton and I knew about it, because Jack told it to me," he said. "So Scott told me to take it out. I didn't want to, but Scott was a successful writer and a writer I respected, so I listened to him and took it out."

Hemingway sat down on the couch and nodded his head sharply a couple of times to be sure he had my attention. "As you get older, it is harder to have heroes, but it is sort of necessary," he said. "I have a cat named Boise, who wants to be a human being," he went on slowly, lowering his voice to a kind of grumble. "So Boise eats everything that human beings eat. He chews Vitamin B Complex capsules, which are as bitter as aloes. He thinks I am holding out on him because I won't give him blood-pressure tablets, and because I let him go to sleep without Seconal." He gave a short, rumbling laugh. "I am a strange old man," he said. "How do you like it now, gentlemen?"

Fifty, Hemingway said, on reconsideration, is not supposed to be old. "It is sort of fun to be fifty and feel you are going to defend the title again," he said. "I won it in the twenties and defended it in the thirties and the forties, and I don't mind at all defending it in the fifties."

After a while, Mrs. Hemingway came into the room. She was wearing gray flannel slacks and a white blouse, and she said she felt wonderful, because she had had her first hot bath in six months. Then she said she was going out to do her errands, and suggested that Hemingway get dressed and go out and do his. He said that it was lunchtime, and that if they went out then, they would have to stop someplace for lunch, whereas if they had lunch sent up to the room, they might save time. Mrs. Hemingway said she would order lunch while he got dressed. Still holding his glass, he reluctantly got up from the couch. Then he finished his drink and went into the bedroom. By the time he came out—wearing the same outfit as the day before, except for a blue shirt with a button-down collar—a waiter had set the table for our lunch. We couldn't have lunch without a bottle of Tavel, Hemingway said, and we waited until the waiter had brought it before starting to eat.

Hemingway began with oysters, and he chewed each one very thoroughly. "Eat good and digest good," he told us.

"Papa, please get glasses fixed," Mrs. Hemingway said.

He nodded. Then he nodded a few times at me—a

repetition of the sign for attention. "What I want to be when I am old is a wise old man who won't bore," he said, then paused while the waiter set a plate of asparagus and an artichoke before him and poured the Tavel. Hemingway tasted the wine and gave the waiter a nod. "I'd like to see all the new fighters, horses, ballets, bike riders, dames, bullfighters, painters, airplanes, sons of bitches, café characters, big international whores, restaurants, years of wine, newsreels, and never have to write a line about any of it," he said. "I'd like to write lots of letters to my friends and get back letters. Would like to be able to make love good until I was eighty-five, the way Clemenceau could. And what I would like to be is not Bernie Baruch. I wouldn't sit on park benches, although I might go around the park once in a while to feed the pigeons, and also I wouldn't have any long beard, so there could be an old man didn't look like Shaw." He stopped and ran the back of his hand along his beard, and looked around the room reflectively. "Have never met Mr. Shaw," he said. "Never been to Niagara Falls, either. Anyway, I would take up harness racing. You aren't up near the top at that until you're over seventy-five. Then I could get me a good young ball club, maybe, like Mr. Mack. Only, I wouldn't signal with a program, so as to break the pattern. Haven't figured out yet what I would signal with. And when that's over, I'll make the prettiest corpse since Pretty Boy Floyd. Only suckers worry about saving their souls. Who the hell should care about saving his soul when it is a man's duty to lose it intelligently, the way you would sell a position you were defending, if you could not hold it, as expensively as possible, trying to make it the most expensive position that was ever sold. It isn't hard to die." He opened his mouth and laughed, at first soundlessly and then loudly. "No more worries," he said. He picked up a long spear of asparagus with his fingers and looked at it without enthusiasm. "It takes a pretty good man to make any sense when he's dying," he said.

Mrs. Hemingway had finished eating, and she quickly finished her wine. Hemingway slowly finished his. I looked at my wristwatch, and found that it was almost three. The waiter started clearing the table, and we all got up. Hemingway stood looking sadly at the bottle of champagne, which was not yet empty. Mrs. Hemingway put on her coat, and I put on mine.

"The half bottle of champagne is the enemy of man," Hemingway said. We all sat down again.

"If I have any money, I can't think of any better way of spending money than on champagne," Hemingway said, pouring some.

When the champagne was gone, we left the suite. Downstairs, Mrs. Hemingway told us to remember to get glasses fixed, and scooted away.

Hemingway balked for a moment in front of the hotel. It was a cool, cloudy day. This was not good weather for him to be out in, he said sulkily, adding that his throat felt kind of sore. I asked him if he wanted to see a doctor. He said no. "I never trust a doctor I have to pay," he said, and started across Fifth Avenue. A flock of pigeons flew by. He stopped, looked up, and aimed an imaginary rifle at them. He pulled the trigger, and then looked disappointed. "Very difficult shot," he said. He turned quickly and pretended to shoot again. "Easy shot," he said. "Look!" He pointed to a spot on the pavement. He seemed to be feeling better, but not much better.

I asked him if he wanted to stop first at his optician's. He said no. I mentioned the coat. He shrugged. Mrs. Hemingway had suggested that he look for a coat at

Abercrombie & Fitch, so I mentioned Abercrombie & Fitch. He shrugged again and lumbered slowly over to a taxi, and we started down Fifth Avenue in the afternoon traffic. At the corner of Fifty-fourth, we stopped on a signal from the traffic cop. Hemingway growled. "I love to see an Irish cop being cold," he said. "Give you eight to one he was an M.P. in the war. Very skillful cop. Feints and fakes good. Cops are not like they are in the Hellinger movies. Only once in a while." We started up again, and he showed me where he once walked across Fifth Avenue with Scott Fitzgerald. "Scott wasn't at Princeton any more, but he was still talking football," he said, without animation. "The ambition of Scott's life was to be on the football team. I said, 'Scott, why don't you cut out this football?' I said, 'Come on, boy.' He said, 'You're crazy.' That's the end of that story. If you can't get through traffic, how the hell are you gonna get through the line? But I am not Thomas Mann," he added. "Get another opinion."

By the time we reached Abercrombie's, Hemingway was moody again. He got out of the taxi reluctantly, and reluctantly entered the store. I asked him whether he wanted to look at a coat first or something else.

"Coat," he said unhappily.

In the elevator, Hemingway looked even bigger and bulkier than he had before, and his face had the expression of a man who is being forcibly subjected to the worst kind of misery. A middle-aged woman standing next to him stared at his scraggly white beard with obvious alarm and disapproval. "Good Christ!" Hemingway said suddenly, in the silence of the elevator, and the middle-aged woman looked down at her feet.

The doors opened at our floor, and we got out and headed for a rack of topcoats. A tall, dapper clerk approached us, and Hemingway shoved his hands into his pants pockets and crouched forward. "I think I still have credit in this joint," he said to the clerk.

The clerk cleared his throat. "Yes, sir," he said.

"Want to see coat," Hemingway said menacingly.

"Yes, sir," said the clerk. "What kind of coat did you wish to see, sir?"

"That one." He pointed to a straight-hanging, beltless tan gabardine coat on the rack. The clerk helped him into it and gently drew him over to a full-length mirror. "Hangs like a shroud," Hemingway said, tearing the coat off. "I'm tall on top. Got any other coat?" he asked, as though he expected the answer to be no. He edged impatiently toward the elevators.

"How about this one, sir, with a removable lining, sir?" the clerk said. This one had a belt. Hemingway tried it on, studied himself in the mirror, and then raised his arms as though he were aiming a rifle. "You going to use it for *shooting,* sir?" the clerk asked. Hemingway grunted, and said he would take the coat. He gave the clerk his name, and the clerk snapped his fingers. "Of course!" he said. "There was *something . . .*" Hemingway looked embarrassed and said to send the coat to him at the Sherry-Netherland, and then said he'd like to look at a belt.

"What kind of belt, Mr. Hemingway?" the clerk asked.

"Guess a brown one," Hemingway said.

We moved over to the belt counter, and another clerk appeared.

"Will you show Mr. Hemingway a belt?" the first clerk said, and stepped back and thoughtfully watched Hemingway.

The second clerk took a tape measure from his pocket, saying he thought Hemingway was a size 44 or 46.

"Wanta bet?" Hemingway asked. He took the clerk's hand and punched himself in the stomach with it.

"Gee, he's got a hard tummy," the belt clerk said. He measured Hemingway's waistline. "Thirty-eight!" he reported. "Small waist for your size. What do you do—a lot of exercise?"

Hemingway hunched his shoulders, feinted, laughed, and looked happy for the first time since we'd left the hotel. He punched himself in the stomach with his own fist.

"Where you going—to Spain again?" the belt clerk asked.

"To Italy," Hemingway said, and punched himself in the stomach again. After Hemingway had decided on a brown calf belt, the clerk asked him whether he wanted a money belt. He said no—he kept his money in a checkbook.

Our next stop was the shoe department, and there Hemingway asked a clerk for some folding bedroom slippers.

"Pullman slippers," the clerk said. "What size?"

" 'Levens," Hemingway said bashfully. The slippers

were produced, and he told the clerk he would take them. "I'll put them in my pocket," he said. "Just mark them, so they won't think I'm a shoplifter."

"You'd be surprised what's taken from the store," said the clerk, who was very small and very old. "Why, the other morning, someone on the first floor went off with a big roulette wheel. Just picked it up and—"

Hemingway was not listening. "Wolfie!" he shouted at a man who seemed almost seven feet tall and whose back was to us.

The man turned around. He had a big, square red face, and at the sight of Hemingway it registered extreme joy. "Papa!" he shouted.

The big man and Hemingway embraced and pounded each other on the back for quite some time. It was Winston Guest. Mr. Guest told us he was going upstairs to pick up a gun, and proposed that we come along. Hemingway asked what kind of gun, and Guest said a ten-gauge magnum.

"Beautiful gun," Hemingway said, taking his bedroom slippers from the clerk and stuffing them into his pocket.

In the elevator, Hemingway and Guest checked with

each other on how much weight they had lost. Guest said he was now down to two hundred and thirty-five, after a good deal of galloping around on polo ponies. Hemingway said he was down to two hundred and eight, after shooting ducks in Cuba and working on his book.

"How's the book now, Papa?" Guest asked as we got out of the elevator.

Hemingway gave his fist-to-the-face laugh and said he was going to defend his title once more. "Wolfie, all of a sudden I found I could write wonderful again, instead of just biting on the nail," he said slowly. "I think it took a while for my head to get rebuilt inside. You should not, ideally, break a writer's head open or give him seven concussions in two years or break six ribs on him when he is forty-seven or push a rear-view-mirror support through the front of his skull opposite the pituitary gland, or, really, shoot at him too much. On the other hand, Wolfie, leave the sons of bitches alone and they are liable to start crawling back into the womb or somewhere if you drop a porkpie hat." He exploded into laughter.

Guest's huge frame shook with almost uncontrollable

laughter. "God, Papa!" he said. "I still have your shooting clothes out at the island. When are you coming out to shoot, Papa?"

Hemingway laughed again and pounded him on the back. "Wolfie, you're so damn big!" he said.

Guest arranged to have his gun delivered, and then we all got into the elevator, the two of them talking about a man who caught a black marlin last year that weighed a thousand and six pounds.

"How do you like it now, gentlemen?" Hemingway asked.

"God, Papa!" said Guest.

On the ground floor, Guest pointed to a mounted elephant head on the wall. "Pygmy elephant, Papa," he said.

"Miserable elephant," said Hemingway.

Their arms around each other, they went out to the street. I said that I had to leave, and Hemingway told me to be sure to come over to the hotel early the next morning, so that I could go with him and Patrick to the Metropolitan Museum. As I walked off, I heard Guest say, "God, Papa, I'm not ashamed of anything I've ever done."

"Nor, oddly enough, am I," said Hemingway.

I looked around. They were punching each other in the stomach and laughing raucously.

———

The following morning, the door of the Hemingway suite was opened for me by Patrick, a shy young man of medium height, with large eyes and a sensitive face. He was wearing gray flannel slacks, a white shirt open at the collar, Argyle socks, and loafers. Mrs. Hemingway was writing a letter at the desk. As I came in, she looked up and said, "As soon as Papa has finished dressing, we're going to look at pictures." She went back to her letter.

Patrick told me that he'd just as soon spend the whole day looking at pictures, and that he had done a bit of painting himself. "Papa has to be back here for lunch with Mr. Scribner," he said, and added that he himself was going to stay in town until the next morning, when the Hemingways sailed. The telephone rang and he answered it. "Papa, I think it's Gigi calling you!" he shouted into the bedroom.

Hemingway emerged, in shirtsleeves, and went to the phone. "How are you, kid?" he said into it, then asked Gigi to come down to the Finca for his next vacation.

"You're welcome down there, Gigi," he said. "You know that cat you liked? The one you named Smelly? We renamed him Ecstasy. Every one of our cats knows his own name." After hanging up, he told me that Gigi was a wonderful shot—that when he was eleven he had won second place in the shoot championship of Cuba. "Isn't that the true gen, Mouse?" he asked.

"That's right, Papa," said Patrick.

I wanted to know what "true gen" meant, and Hemingway explained that it was British slang for "information," from "intelligence." "It's divided into three classes: gen; the true gen, which is as true as you can state it; and the really true gen, which you can operate on," he said.

He looked at the green orchids. "*My* mother never sent *me* any flowers," he said. His mother was about eighty, he said, and lived in River Forest, Illinois. His father, who was a physician, had been dead for many years; he shot himself when Ernest was a boy. "Let's get going if we're going to see the pictures," he said. "I told Charlie Scribner to meet me here at one. Excuse me while I wash. In big city, I guess you wash your neck." He went back into the bedroom. While he was gone, Mrs. Hemingway told me that Ernest was the second of six children—Marcelline, then Ernest, Ursula, Madelaine, Carol, and the youngest, his only brother, Leicester. All the sisters were named after saints. Every one of the children was married; Leicester was living in Bogotá, Colombia, where he was attached to the United States Embassy.

Hemingway came out in a little while, wearing his new coat. Mrs. Hemingway and Patrick put on their coats, and we went downstairs. It was raining, and we hurried into a taxi. On the way to the Metropolitan, Hemingway said very little; he just hummed to himself and watched the street. Mrs. Hemingway told me that he was usually unhappy in taxis, because he could not sit in the front seat to watch the road ahead. He looked out the window and pointed to a flock of birds flying across the sky. "In this town, birds fly, but they're not serious about it," he said. "New York birds don't climb."

When we drew up at the Museum entrance, a line of schoolchildren was moving in slowly. Hemingway impatiently led us past them. In the lobby, he paused, pulled a silver flask from one of his coat pockets, unscrewed its top, and took a long drink. Putting the flask back in his pocket, he asked Mrs. Hemingway whether she wanted to see the Goyas first or the Breughels. She said the Breughels.

"I learned to write by looking at paintings in the Luxembourg Museum in Paris," he said. "I never went past high school. When you've got a hungry gut and the museum is free, you go to the museum. Look," he said, stopping before "Portrait of a Man," which has been attributed to both Titian and Giorgione. "They were old Venice boys, too."

"Here's what I like, Papa," Patrick said, and Hemingway joined his son in front of "Portrait of Federigo Gonzaga (1500–1540)," by Francesco Francia. It shows, against a landscape, a small boy with long hair and a cloak.

"This is what we try to do when we write, Mousie," Hemingway said, pointing to the trees in the background. "We always have this in when we write."

Mrs. Hemingway called to us. She was looking at "Portrait of the Artist," by Van Dyck. Hemingway looked at it, nodded approval, and said, "In Spain, we had a fighter pilot named Whitey Dahl, so Whitey came to me one time and said, 'Mr. Hemingway, is Van Dyck a good painter?' I said, 'Yes, he is.' He said, 'Well, I'm glad, because I have one in my room and I like it very much, and I'm glad he's a good painter because I like him.' The next day, Whitey was shot down."

We all walked over to Rubens' "The Triumph of Christ Over Sin and Death." Christ is shown surrounded by snakes and angels and is being watched by a figure in a cloud. Mrs. Hemingway and Patrick said they thought it didn't look like the usual Rubens.

"Yeah, he did that all right," Hemingway said authoritatively. "You can tell the real just as a bird dog can tell. Smell them. Or from having lived with very poor but very good painters."

That settled that, and we went on to the Breughel room. It was closed, we discovered. The door bore a sign that read "NOW UNDERTAKING REPAIRS."

"They have our indulgence," Hemingway said, and took another drink from his flask. "I sure miss the good Breughel," he said as we moved along. "It's the great one, of the harvesters. It is a lot of people cutting grain, but he uses the grain geometrically, to make an emotion that is so strong for me that I can hardly take it." We came to El Greco's green "View of Toledo" and stood looking at it a long time. "This is the best picture in the Museum for me, and Christ knows there are some lovely ones," Hemingway said.

Patrick admired several paintings Hemingway didn't approve of. Every time this happened, Hemingway got into an involved technical discussion with his son. Patrick would shake his head and laugh and say he respected Hemingway's opinions. He didn't argue much. "What the hell!" Hemingway said suddenly. "I don't want to be an art critic. I just want to look at pictures and be happy with them and learn from them. Now, this for me is a damn good picture." He stood back and peered at a Reynolds entitled "Colonel George Coussmaker," which shows the Colonel leaning against a tree and holding his horse's bridle. "Now, this Colonel is a son of a bitch who was willing to pay money to the best portrait painter of his day just to have himself painted," Hemingway said, and gave a short laugh. "Look at the man's arrogance and the strength in the neck of the horse and the way the man's legs hang. He's so arrogant he can afford to lean against a tree."

We separated for a while and looked at paintings individually, and then Hemingway called us over and pointed to a picture labelled, in large letters, "Catharine

Lorillard Wolfe" and, in small ones, "By Cabanel." "This is where I got confused as a kid, in Chicago," he said. "My favorite painters for a long time were Bunte and Ryerson, two of the biggest and wealthiest families in Chicago. I always thought the names in big letters were the painters."

After we reached the Cézannes and Degas and the other Impressionists, Hemingway became more and more excited, and discoursed on what each artist could do and how and what he had learned from each. Patrick listened respectfully and didn't seem to want to talk about painting techniques any more. Hemingway spent several minutes looking at Cézanne's "Rocks—Forest of Fontainebleau." "This is what we try to do in writing, this and this, and the woods, and the rocks we have to climb over," he said. "Cézanne is my painter, after the early painters. Wonder, wonder painter. Degas was another wonder painter. I've never seen a bad Degas. You know what he did with the bad Degas? He burned them."

Hemingway took another long drink from his flask. We came to Manet's pastel portrait of Mlle. Valtesse de la Bigne, a young woman with blond hair coiled on the top of her head. Hemingway was silent for a while, looking at it; finally he turned away. "Manet could show the bloom people have when they're still innocent and before they've been disillusioned," he said.

As we walked along, Hemingway said to me, "I can make a landscape like Mr. Paul Cézanne. I learned how to make a landscape from Mr. Paul Cézanne by walking through the Luxembourg Museum a thousand times with an empty gut, and I am pretty sure that if Mr. Paul was around, he would like the way I make them and be happy that I learned it from him." He had learned a lot from Mr. Johann Sebastian Bach, too. "In the first paragraphs of 'Farewell,' I used the word 'and' consciously over and over the way Mr. Johann Sebastian Bach used a note in music when he was emitting counterpoint. I can almost write like Mr. Johann sometimes—or, anyway, so he would like it. All such people are easy to deal with, because we all know you have to learn."

"Papa, look at this," Patrick said. He was looking at "Meditation on the Passion," by Carpaccio. Patrick said it had a lot of strange animals in it for a religious painting.

"Huh!" Hemingway said. "Those painters always put the sacred scenes in the part of Italy they liked best or where they came from or where their girls came from. They made their girls the Madonnas. This is supposed to be Palestine, and Palestine is a long way off, he figures. So he puts in a red parrot, and he puts in deer and a leopard. And then he thinks, This is the Far East and it's far away. So he puts in the Moors, the traditional enemy of the Venetians." He paused and looked to see what else the painter had put in his picture. "Then he gets hungry, so he puts in rabbits," he said. "Goddam, Mouse, we saw a lot of good pictures. Mouse, don't you think two hours is a long time looking at pictures?"

Everybody agreed that two hours was a long time looking at pictures, so Hemingway said that we would skip the Goyas, and that we would all go to the Museum again when they returned from Europe.

It was still raining when we came out of the Museum. "Goddam, I hate to go out in the rain," Hemingway said. "Goddam, I hate to get wet."

———

Charles Scribner was waiting in the lobby of the hotel. "Ernest," he said, shaking Hemingway's hand. He was a dignified, solemn, slow-speaking gentleman with silvery hair.

"We've been looking at pictures, Charlie," Hemingway said as we went up in the elevator. "They have some pretty good pictures now, Charlie."

Scribner nodded and said, "Yuh, yuh."

"Was fun for country boy like me," Hemingway said.

"Yuh, yuh," said Scribner.

We went into the suite and took off our coats, and Hemingway said we would have lunch right there. He called room service, and Mrs. Hemingway sat down at the desk to finish her letter. Hemingway sat down on the couch with Mr. Scribner and began telling him that he had been jamming, like a rider in a six-day bike race, and Patrick sat quietly in a corner and watched his father. The waiter came in and passed out menus. Scribner said he was going to order the most expensive item on the menu, because Hemingway was paying for it. He laughed tentatively, and Patrick laughed to keep him company. The waiter retired with our orders, and Scribner and Hemingway talked business for a while. Scribner wanted to know whether Hemingway had the letters he had written to him.

Hemingway said, "I carry them everyplace I go, Charlie, together with a copy of the poems of Robert Browning."

Scribner nodded and, from the inner pocket of his jacket, took some papers—copies of the contract for the new book, he said. The contract provided for an advance of twenty-five thousand dollars against royalties, beginning at fifteen per cent.

Hemingway signed the contract, and got up from the couch. Then he said, "Never ran as no genius, but I'll defend the title again against all the good young new ones." He lowered his head, put his left foot forward, and jabbed at the air with a left and a right. "Never let them hit you solid," he said.

Scribner wanted to know where Hemingway could be reached in Europe. Care of the Guaranty Trust Company in Paris, Hemingway told him. "When we took Paris, I tried to take that bank and got smacked back," he said, and laughed a shy laugh. "I thought it would be awfully nice if I could take my own bank."

"Yuh, yuh," Scribner said. "What are you planning to do in Italy, Ernest?"

Hemingway said he would work part of each day and see his Italian friends and go duckhunting in the mornings. "We shot three hundred and thirty-one ducks to six guns there one morning," he said. "Mary shot good, too."

Mrs. Hemingway looked up. "Any girl who marries Papa has to learn how to carry a gun," she said, and returned to her letter-writing.

"I went hunting once in Suffolk, England," Scribner said. Everyone waited politely for him to continue. "I remember they gave me goose eggs to eat for breakfast in Suffolk. Then we went out to shoot. I didn't know how to get my gun off safe."

"Hunting is sort of a good life," Hemingway said. "Better than Westport or Bronxville, I think."

"After I learned how to get my gun off safe, I couldn't hit anything," Scribner said.

"I'd like to make the big Monte Carlo shoot and the Championship of the World at San Remo," Hemingway said. "I'm in pretty good shape to shoot either one. It's not a spectator sport at all. But exciting to do and wonderful to manage. I used to handle Wolfie in big shoots. He is a great shot. It was like handling a great horse."

"I finally got one," Scribner said timidly.

"Got what?" asked Hemingway.

"A rabbit," Scribner said. "I shot this rabbit."

"They haven't held the big Monte Carlo shoot since 1939," Hemingway said. "Only two Americans ever won it in seventy-four years. Shooting gives me a good feeling. A lot of it is being together and friendly instead of feeling you are in some place where everybody hates you and wishes you ill. It is faster than baseball, and you are out on one strike."

The telephone rang, and Hemingway picked it up, listened, said a few words, and then turned to us and said that an outfit called Endorsements, Inc., had offered him four thousand dollars to pose as a Man of Distinction. "I told them I wouldn't drink the stuff for four thousand dollars," he said. "I told them I was a champagne man. Am trying to be a good guy, but it's a difficult trade. What you win in Boston, you lose in Chicago."

—1950

AFTERWORD

One of the earliest of my privileged friendships that developed with people I've written about was with Ernest
Hemingway and his wife, Mary. In 1950—when he was,
as he liked to put it, "half a century old"—I wrote a long
Profile about him in *The New Yorker,* and after it appeared, I didn't understand why some people were almost deliriously censorious about the way Hemingway
talked and the way he enjoyed himself and the way he
was openly vulnerable. By now—having the advantage
of years of friendship with the Hemingways after the
publication of the Profile—I've gained some insight into
that peculiar response to him.

I once wrote, in an Introduction to an edition of my book *Reporting:* "Anyone who trusts you enough to talk about himself to you is giving you a form of friendship.... If you spend weeks or months with someone, not only taking his time and energy but entering into his life, you naturally become his friend. A friend is not to be used and abandoned; the friendship established in writing about someone often continues to grow after what has been written is published." That's the way I like it to be for me.

As a friend, Hemingway was stalwart. He had told me to feel free to write whatever I chose to write about him, and he never reneged. "I thought your piece was a good, straight OK piece," he said about the Profile initially. A week later, he said: "Don't ever worry about loseing"— it was his habit to keep the "e" in his participles—"me friends nor anything about piece." He added, "I take the wind like an old tree; have felt the wind before; north south east and west." Another time he said that he lost about a friend a day over the Profile. "But what the hell; any friend you can lose you might as well lose them early and anyway it is too late." Once he said: "Please don't think you ever have to answer any jerks or ever defend me. I am self-propelled and self-defendable." And again: "Actually good old Profile made me about as many enemies as we have in North Korea. But who gives a shit? A man should be known by the enemies he keeps." Several years later, he told me that people continued to talk to him about the Profile: "All are very astonished because I don't hold anything against you who made an effort to destroy me and nearly did, they say. I always tell them how can I be destroyed by a woman when she is a friend of mine and we have never even been to bed and no money has changed hands?"

He had some succinct advice for me as a writer: "Just call them the way you see them and the hell with it."

———

Throughout the succeeding eleven years, until his death, Hemingway wrote scores of letters to me. Mary also wrote from time to time. An unshakable friendship developed, and Hemingway called our correspondence "the best invention since penicillin." He paid me what I considered the ultimate compliment, when he said, "I know you will stick like the Third or Fourth Infantry Divisions." I last heard from him in 1961—fourteen years after we met—when he was in St. Mary's Hospital in Rochester, Minnesota, where he had gone to seek med-

ical help. It was about five months before he killed himself, in Ketchum. After that, I would see his wife, Mary,
from time to time, especially when she came to live in
New York, until her death in 1986.

In his letters to me, Hemingway often used the joke
"Indian" talk he had invented in conversation with his
wife and friends, dropping his articles and being inten-
tionally ungrammatical. He knew that time was short
("Time is the least thing we have of," as he says in the
Profile) so he devised a way of talking that was free and
loose and full of his own kind of shorthand. He kidded
around in other ways, too. For example, while writing a
letter he would switch from typewriter to handwriting:
"Had to quit typing due to my self pity + cramps. There
are a lot of compensations in life. Anyhow, I don't have
to re-marry Dorothy Parker. Please write. Huck Hemingstein." Or: "Wrote you a funny letter last night when
yours came. But had to tear it up because it was too
rough. I shouldn't have said that about the sin house, etc.
anyway. But I got used to telling the truth to you and it's
a hell of a habit to stop. Probably am just as much of a
jerk as those bastards that rush to their analysts. My analyst's name is Royal Portable (noiseless) the 3rd." He

also liked to refer to his typewriter as the Royal Deportable Machine.

Hemingway signed a few of his letters "Papa," but mostly he signed them "Ernest" or "Honest Ernie" or "Huck von Hemingstein" or "Ernest Buck Hemingstein" or "Mountain Boy Huck" or "Huckmanship von Hemingstein" or "Love and good luck, Ernest." Or, after signing, he would draw three mountain peaks, which I assumed was his own idea of an Indian sign.

Occasionally, he would apologize for his "sloppy writing." And he would ask, "But you don't want me to write all the time with a hard, gem-like flame do you?" Then he would throw in a Hemingway sentence as only Hemingway could write it. In talking about the "haunted, nocturnal life" he led in Cuba, he once wrote that he had been up since "0230" and it was now "0530": "It is getting light now before the sun rises and the hills are grey from the dew of last night."

From Cuba, he often wrote once or twice a week. When he went to Spain or to Africa, the letters would come less frequently. Each time I opened one of them on onionskin stationery with "FINCA VIGIA, SAN FRANCISCO DE PAULA, CUBA" printed across the top, I felt the thrill of knowing that it was from Hemingway. Every letter contained electric echoes of the writer I had discovered at the age of eleven, when I found *The Sun Also Rises,* a forbidden book, under my brother Simeon's pillow. As Joan Didion wrote last year in *The New Yorker:* "This is the man to whom words mattered." I might not have completely understood the novel, but the words—complete sentences—stayed in my consciousness as no words ever have. It was in Hemingway's writing that I first learned about clarity and simplicity and the beauty of unadorned prose. It was from his fiction that I learned how to try to write fact.

A couple of times the Hemingways and I planned to meet in Paris, but we didn't connect, so we got together during their few visits to New York. Despite many invitations from Hemingway and his wife to come and stay with them in Cuba, I never visited them there. I've never felt comfortable "visiting" most people. Besides, I didn't want to spoil our particular equation.

In Hemingway's letters to me, he ridiculed people he didn't respect; he gossiped about people he knew; he sympathized with people who were in trouble. He told of his impatience with the wife of one of his friends.

"There was always, with her, a lot of stuff about being Jewish and not being Jewish," he said. "This always bores the hell out of me because I would just as soon observe Yom Kippur as Easter, and I am really an Indian I guess anyway, and we probably were as badly bitched as the Jews. I like Jews very much, but I always get bored with people making a career of their race, religion, or their noble families. Why can't we take the whole damned thing for granted?"

In another letter he said, "I usually introduce myself as Hemingstein when meeting known anti-Semites and their friends. But actually the name is Hemingway, and there is nothing I can do about it."

—

Hemingway liked to make lists, and when he listed the people he loved he usually started with the names of his sons: John (nicknamed Bumby), Patrick (nicknamed Mousie), and Gregory (nicknamed Gigi). Next, he would affectionately list all his wives: Hadley, Pauline, Martha, and Mary. (He described Pauline as a fine woman after she had visited them at Finca Vigia.) When John became a captain of infantry in Germany, Hemingway proudly told me, "He is a nice boy and I love him very much and he loves me. Since have never been on a couch don't know whether there is anything wrong with that."

Eventually, we would tell each other about our personal lives. I told the Hemingways about my romance with William Shawn, the editor of *The New Yorker,* which began shortly after the Profile was published and continued in late 1951, after my return from eighteen months in Hollywood, where I had gone in an effort to disentangle myself from this turn in my life. The Hemingways were very sympathetic and supportive in my efforts to escape from the involvement—the love story that I described in my 1998 book *Here But Not Here.* The Hemingways had sensed my situation, and both of them tactfully offered some help. Mary wrote me a sweet letter with some practical maxims, which were diplomatically vetoed by her husband. It turned out, of course, that the romance was inescapable, and it continued happily for forty years—until William Shawn's death in 1992.

I told Hemingway that my father was a Socialist, that he had voted for Eugene Victor Debs. He replied that Debs was the only candidate he had ever voted for. He wrote to me about various incidents along the line: He told me how he had hurt himself in a fall on his boat in

Cuba, on a three-day fishing trip, in a heavy sea; he'd gone up to the flying bridge, slipped, fell, and sustained a cut on his skull that required "only three stitches." He would keep me posted on slight changes in Mary's routine. "Mary had her hair cut short," he would say. "She had hers long when everyone else had it short. But I like it very much both ways." He reported happily that he had all his taxes paid for 1951 and 1952. In the mid 1950s, Hemingway said that he "was starting to get very happy about going to Africa." "It certainly will be nice to talk Swahili and have the nights cold and get up before daylight and see the Southern Cross when you go to the latrine and sleep nights good from walking in the hills," he said. When their small plane crashed while flying over the Belgian Congo, they wrote me that they were happy to be alive, although they had a collection of un-catalogued aches and pains. Hemingway, Mary said, took the worst jolts to his liver and kidneys.

In addition to being marvellously eclectic, the letters were full of facts. Hemingway *told* me things. I found skiing difficult, for example, and the proliferation of broken legs among skiers scared me. "Nobody has any real strength in their legs anymore, because they don't climb," he said. "Skiing is all on a ski-lift basis. . . . They don't know the mountains."

He didn't feel that he had to conceal his romantic notions about the military life. He would tell me, "I wish we could go to war (shoot-shoot war) sometime with Buck Lanham and Chink Dorman-Smith." Lanham, his best friend, was commander of the Twenty-second Infantry Regiment. "You'd have fun. It is supposed to be a terrible sin to have fun in war. But we commit it and the three of us are very light-hearted people when the chips are down."

I didn't go fishing or shooting or hunting or camping or trekking on safaris to Africa—much less to war. I had no interest in doing any of that. But I enjoyed hearing Hemingway talk about all those things, because he said everything with originality, with zest, with energy, and with humor. During one fishing trip, he reported to me that they had caught five marlin, five tuna, five kingfish, about a dozen barracuda, a very big grouper, and a big female dolphin, "the kind that change from gold to silver when they die." He liked to instruct me in the ways of the porpoise and the whale. The porpoise, he said, is your best friend at sea; he will stay with you and play for miles and come around the boat and blow at night like a whale but without a whale's terrible stink. The sperm whale, I learned, when he's been eating squid, has the worst halitosis. Some of the fishing talk would keep me from eating seafood for months at a time.

Sometimes he described how he felt about the Finca. On returning there from a trip, he would say that it was even better than he remembered. It was wonderful, he said, "to have lots of room to work and plenty of big waste baskets." No one else told me things like that.

Occasionally, Mary would write a letter: "Jupiter (Here we pronounce him Hoopiter) is blazing in the eastern sky off the front porch, in spite of all the windows open, the house is domesticated with the smell of freshly baked bread which I just took out of the oven; Papa is writing a letter in the library and the dogs wander back and front between us knowing very well that it is time for us to be eating dinner; the magnum, or is it jerobam, is sitting unopened, waiting an occasion worthy of it, and all evening I have been wishing, really, that you were here…"

In our letters, we also discussed some of my enthusiasms. For example, he tutored me on the poker fundamentals. Never call; either raise or throw down. Play your good cards for keeps when you hold them and ride out your bad ones. Also, don't come in on every pot. As for tennis, he told me that he used to play a lot of singles with his third wife, Martha Gellhorn. "You had to let her *almost* win for her to be happy," he said. "If you let her win, she became insufferable."

———

When we talked about writing or writers, it wasn't in a strictly intellectual idiom. In connection with the fish, we once got on to the subject of *Moby Dick*. I remember that I told him I liked reading the book. He said, "It is all wonderful except the rhetoric, which is shit. Also it is a lot of words about a whale. But in it there is something wonderful." Then, in his metaphorical habit of comparing writers to baseball pitchers, he said that Melville is like a "truly good left-hand pitcher with no control but who has played with every club and knows everything."

Hemingway could be very funny about other writers. "What is Faulkner's book like?" he once asked me. "Did you read it? I mustn't comment on it until I have read it or failed to be able to read it, but one thing I know is that writing would sure be easy if you went up in a barn with a quart of whiskey and wrote five thousand words on a good day without syntax." Once he asked me what I thought of

Faulkner's "ranking of American writers." He considered this an appalling practice. "They are all ranking each other now," he said. "Like in J. Arthur Ranking Service."

From time to time, I would ask Hemingway what he thought of this or that piece of writing. When Shirley Jackson's famous short story "The Lottery" was published in *The New Yorker*, in 1948, I admired it, and I asked Hemingway to read it. He replied, "That story was a stinker." He called the ending "faked and phony," adding, "You have to write so people believe it." He said it was "the worst story I ever read in *The New Yorker*."

I liked Norman Mailer's *The Naked and the Dead* and sent it to Hemingway. He thought that Mailer was very skillful and said he was "all for him." He went on, "I wish him luck and that he keeps on writing. He has lots of stuff." Another time he wrote of Mailer, "He has a fine imagination and if he disciplines it and controls it and invents truly from what he really knows, he can be a hell of a writer. Don't tell him this as kids resent even an opinion." He thought Irwin Shaw was "a jerk and a good short-story writer. But if I'd say he was a bad playwright (which he is) he would say I was anti-Semitic." He called Dawn Powell a wonderful writer who "has everything that Dotty Parker is supposed to have and is not tear-stained." He told me that Thurber was a better writer than Benchley. Once I took my great colleague Joe Mitchell (that other fish enthusiast) to meet him, and thereafter Hemingway always said how much he liked Mitchell's "The Bottom of the Harbor." At their meeting, they were initially uncomfortable with each other, but then they found common ground in their shared feelings of sympathy for Ingrid Bergman, who was experiencing hostile press accounts of her relationship with Roberto Rossellini. Hemingway criticized *The New Yorker* for "not being stapled well." He complained that the magazine fell to pieces and he had to fit it all together to read what he now and then crankily called "the dullest features in the world."

When Hemingway liked or admired a bullfighter or a boxer or a writer or a cook, he was always generous about sharing the object of his enthusiasm with someone. He was a good friend of Bernard Berenson ("the most intelligent man I know"), and told me, in a letter, "Old Mr. B is 86 plus seven months. He always wants me to be impressed by how old he is and how he might die and I never want to tell him that I don't impress by being old; only by being intelligent and friendly, and that people who have been D plus 104 and finally much worse don't impress at all about going to die."

In 1954, after Hemingway was awarded the Nobel Prize, he said that he and Mary didn't see anybody coming down to Cuba but "bloody bores, ex-rummies and people who want to shake the hand of the man who shook down Alfred Nobel's legatees." He would tell me about people who came up to him and said, "I just wanted to tell you, Mr. Hemingway, that I think you are our greatest writer. You and Louis Bromfield." (That one made me laugh out loud.)

The same year, Hemingway shyly reported to me that another unusual visitor had turned up at the Finca—Ava Gardner. "Only for three days," he said. "She is no strain, and I like to look at beautiful women and will go out in the boat tomorrow with her and Mary and Mayito Menocal. She was pretty good to come down with neither reporters nor cameramen and using the name of Ann Clark."

Mary also kept me posted on the visitors. One April morning in 1955, while Hemingway was working and she was in the pantry making lunch, "Without invitation through the front door came four stalwart sophomores from Princeton—spring vacation is such a fine time to go south—who stayed, swimming in the pool and nibbling and drinking there, until 3 P.M. At 6:30 arrived a Young Writer who wanted criticism and advice . . ." But the Finca, she said, was mighty pleasant—"trees flowering, vines flowering, the pool just cool enough, and you should taste the tomatoes, also our broccoli, green peppers, lima beans and radishes and cauliflower and carrots and Swiss chard and onions and beets and corn and cabbage and especially our Yucca."

Hemingway seemed to enjoy having visitors, but he often wished they would go away and let him work. At the end of one letter, marked "0215" at the top, he wrote, "I am awake for the night after haveing sent everybody to bed. But if you want to know how lonely a man can be when his damn book comes out you could bring down your lonely detector and make some accurate readings."

When Hemingway was feeling bleak, he invariably apologized. "I'm sorry daughter," he wrote, "when I'm not a better example. Nobody ever fielded 1000 if they tried for the hard ones. Nor if they didn't." And he added, "Anyway thanks very much for letter and try and have one here for when we get back. It is nice to come back and have a letter. But don't write if you are working too hard."

He often wrote about the terrible heat, and once said, "Sorry this is such a lousy letter. Did you ever read any of those stories about India and the summer heat when the Monsoon has failed and people go heat nutty and take a rifle out of the racks and shoot somebody in barracks? It has been that hot day and night. Only you can't take any rifle out of the rack and shoot the sergeant. You get up instead and re-write for six hours; copying and re-writing and writing new in long hand until the paper gets so wet it won't take a pencil. Then you stand up and sign checks and business letters and necessary family letters on the typewriter hopeing to get to the pool before the last patch of shade where the water is cool will be gone. That's why you don't write Lillian. It's really been a son of a bitch of a summer. But it's been harder on my black dog who wasn't designed for this climate and I feel guilty about ever haveing brought him here. But he had a fine fall and winter last year and if I would have left him in Ketchum where he chased cars he surely would have been killed. Better stop before I bore you some more."

Some months later, he wrote, "mustn't mind if I'm

sort of beat up just now. Write if you have time. It makes a lot of difference to me."

Hemingway always cheered me on in my writing projects, and he confided in me about his own battles. In 1951, when he was working on *The Old Man and the Sea*, he wrote, "By the time I get it all right and as good as I can do they will probably be dropping atomic bombs around like goat shit. But we can make a trip to some comparatively unbombed area and you can read it in Mss if they have stopped publishing books."

The following spring when he was finishing the book, he was torn, as many writers are, between the need to keep it to himself until it was ready for publication and the temptation to share his excitement over what he was doing. "I've tried to go past the best of whatever I could do best and to see how far you could concentrate on the prose," he said. "But I tried to do it without making any break in a straight simple story. You'll know what you think when you read it. I shouldn't talk about it and I won't. I only say that much because we have been good friends since Ketchum, and I get used to telling you things I don't tell other people, and I forget that when you have a book, you should keep your mouth shut and not say anything you know about it."

When *The Old Man and the Sea* was published, Hemingway told me it was very popular with people in Cuba. He had fun with the way some highbrow critics discussed the "symbolism" in the story. "Down here nobody sees symbolism in it at all," he said. "They think it is about *la puta mar* and an old man and a fish and sharks just the way I wrote it."

His novel and my book *Picture* came out about the same time in 1952. "Well, we both came out of this year OK," he said. "I'm prouder of you than me. But I'm proud of both of us." "When they get this year sorted out," he wrote in another letter, "there will be yours and mine as the straight ones. This is not the sin of pride. It is just telling you what I know. Hope I don't act as though I know too much. But if I don't know about writing by now, I should take up some other form of work. When I get sick of things, I always study navigation or meteorology or do Combat problems for small units or, like tonight, listen to Pablo Casals play Bach."

When he was depressed or discouraged, he sometimes resorted to his baseball or boxing metaphors, saying he was "pitching double headers to empty stands," or "fighting twenty round fights with Stanley Ketchel without a paying customer in the house." Then he added, "Well, Dr., when you are half a hundred years old and know your trade what the hell is the difference under what conditions you practice it?"

At times, he was openly sentimental. Once he told me I was the only American writer he'd heard from on one of his birthdays. "I heard from the young German and Italian writers," he said. "No reason why anyone should say anything on your birthday. But it makes you very pleased when you do hear from somebody." There were times when Hemingway thought nobody "wished him well." But he quickly corrected himself and said that was wrong, that a lot of people wished him well but just didn't, he guessed, tell him about it. Then he might become sadly philosophical and say, "Your legend grows like the barnacles on the bottom of a ship and is about as useful—less useful."

———

There has been a great deal of speculation in the past thirty-eight years about the nature of Hemingway's death. Mary Hemingway said it was an accident, and I believe her. Hemingway was impatient with suicide. He would say, "Don't die. That is the only thing I know is really worthless." He loved and believed in life. When Thomas Heggen, the *Mr. Roberts* playwright, committed suicide, Hemingway said to me, "Now, a guy makes a little money with a play like *Mr. Roberts.* Nothing occurs to him better than to kill himself. You'd think he'd buy himself all the women in the world or go to China or take a good room at the Ritz in Paris and be the Proust of the people. No, he kills himself."

On the same theme, he said, "How people cling to their useless lives I do not understand. Some Africans when they decide to die, just die. I think I understand how they do it, but have always been playing on the other team and engaged in deciding to live when it is actually impossible. Sometimes that is a little rough."

All writers yearn to be considered the best. Some conceal the yearning; others deny it. Hemingway, more than any other writer I've known, was forthright about this wish, and as touching as a child. He told me once that he wanted to be Champion of the World. "But I have that son of a bitch Tolstoi blocking me and when I get by him I run into Shakespeare," he said. "It would be an out to say S. never wrote them. But whoever wrote them is the best writer. The main trouble is that he was in there first and wrote all the things I would have liked to have written and never can ever because he did." He would ask, "What the hell do you do when they wrote it first?"

In rereading Hemingway's letters, written more than four decades ago, I am struck by their modernity. For me, his presence is as alive as his fiction, and I feel blessed to have had his trust and his friendship. I feel now, as I felt when I first got to know him, that he represents the very soul of what we call a writer. And I still believe that he may well be the greatest novelist and short-story writer of our day.

"The only thing for me to do is write good books," Hemingway once said to me after reading a mean piece about his novel *Across the River and into the Trees*, in *Time*. "I may be a no good son of a bitch and lead a highly criticizable life. But I am a good and conscientious writer, and they ought to give you that." Once he speculated about why he had been criticized so often. "I joke all the time at myself, and everybody else and at everything and most literary critics are very solemn and without humor and they resent that," he said.

Hemingway was able to say what I believe to be the truth about the way a great writer feels about his own work: "When I'm going good, don't give a damn about anything nor anybody," he wrote. "People who don't know work is your truest love, feel the thing come between you, and always get jealous and pick fights. Well, I love my work more than I love any woman or anything else."

A NOTE ON THE TYPE

The principal text of this Modern Library edition
was set in a digitized version of Janson,
a typeface that dates from about 1690 and was cut by Nicholas Kis,
a Hungarian working in Amsterdam. The original matrices have
survived and are held by the Stempel foundry in Germany.
Hermann Zapf redesigned some of the weights and sizes for Stempel,
basing his revisions on the original design.